JOHN DURANT is acquiring vast recognition as one of the finest chroniclers of Americana through judicious use of illustrations and text, a strange twist of events for one whose early education was in Wall Street as a member of the New York Stock Exchange.

A Yale graduate (1925), Mr. Durant launched his free-lance writing career on sports and outdoor subjects while he was dealing with stocks and bonds. Service in World War II interrupted his writing when he became seriously occupied as a Lieutenant in the Naval Reserve. He saw action at Tarawa and Kwajelein with an amphibious force.

After the war Mr. Durant and his wife (a co-author on many of his books) took several canoeing trips into the interior of Quebec to gather material for outdoor subjects. Mrs. Durant has done the photography for all her husband's magazine articles and several of his picture books. The Durants live in New Lison, New York — halfway between the New York City and the Canadian border.

Predictions

Predictions

PICTORIAL PREDICTIONS FROM THE PAST

by John Durant

A. S. BARNES AND COMPANY NEW YORK

To Paul MacLean

a good friend

Contents

Introduction

The pictures in this book were culled from numerous publications of the past hundred years whose artists dipped pen and brush into the crystal ball and sketched the events of tomorrow. Often with tongue in cheek these imaginative fellows of the drawing board glimpsed the future but just as often they saw it with clear and sober eyes, recording predictions with astonishing accuracy. As the pages of this volume testify, they foresaw such things as radio, TV, air conditioning in the home, the heavier-than-air flying machine, the automobile and the super highway, farming and rain-making from the clouds, the drive-in church service, the baby incubator, plastic surgery, racial integration in the schoolroom, sky-writing, the pent house apartment, the trailer home, the four-day transatlantic liner, women in military service, prohibition's 'Rum Row,' the rebirth of German militarism in the 1930's (a prediction made in 1918), the engulfment of Europe and Asia by the Russian Bear (a 1904 prediction), and the customs, fashions and foibles of our life today.

Not always were they so right, of course. A notable off-target shot is F. Opper's drawing of Thomas A. Edison which shows the inventor as a fraud who would never perfect his long-promised electric lamp. Another is James Montgomery Flagg's savage cartoon of an all-Negro Harvard football team of the future. There are many other misses here but in the main these artists outguessed the more serious prophets of their day and seemed to have a good time doing it.

This book was done on the side, so to speak, while we were doing research on our other books during the past several years. As we went through the old periodicals page by page we became increasingly fascinated by the number of prophetic illustrations therein. These we noted and later collected to make this volume. It is sincerely hoped that the reader will have as much enjoyment going through it as we did in putting it together.

John Durant

Life Today Through Yesterday's Crystal Ball

1903 PUCK

The mania for speed will dominate life in the Twentieth Century, according to this montage.

The automobile (then only ten years old in America) will be the Exterminator, the great killer on the highways of the future, said *Puck*. Electric trolleys will roar between New York and Chicago in twenty hours; trains will cross the continent in three days; airships will fly to Alaska in a matter of hours and, incredible as it then seemed, steamships will cross the Atlantic in four days.

1877 NEW YORK DAILY GRAPHIC

Uncanny in its accuracy was this cartoon which shows "The Orator of the Future" broadcasting to the four corners of the earth.

NEW YORK IN A FEW YEARS FROM NOW.

1881 HARPER'S WEEKLY

When cartoonist Thomas Nast drew this sketch of New York's future sky-line in 1881 Trinity Church steeple was the highest point in the city (and so remained until 1893 when a 17-story building was erected in lower Manhattan). Trinity Church can be seen in this remarkable pen-and-ink forecast in the center of the sketch, engulfed by towering buildings on all sides—which, of course, is exactly what has happened.

1901 LIFE

This picture predicted with some degree of accuracy the modern superhighway and the consternation that would take place if a horse and wagon
should ever appear upon it. (America's first express highway was the
Bronx River Parkway, opened in 1925.)

1899 LIFE

The Twentieth Century, according to cartoonist F. W. Read, will see a bridge spanning the Atlantic upon which trolleys will ply between New York and London in seven hours.

1903 LIFE

When this illustration appeared in 1903 wireless telegraphy was a novelty, the first official transatlantic telegram having been sent only the year before. Ship-to-shore messages were yet to come. When they do arrive, mused *Life,* think of the terrors ahead for the steamship passenger. He will be plagued by a swarm of troublesome messages, among them calls for margin by his stock broker. In 1929, the year of the great stock market crash (26 years after this picture appeared), the oceanic air was indeed filled with frantic messages from Wall Street.

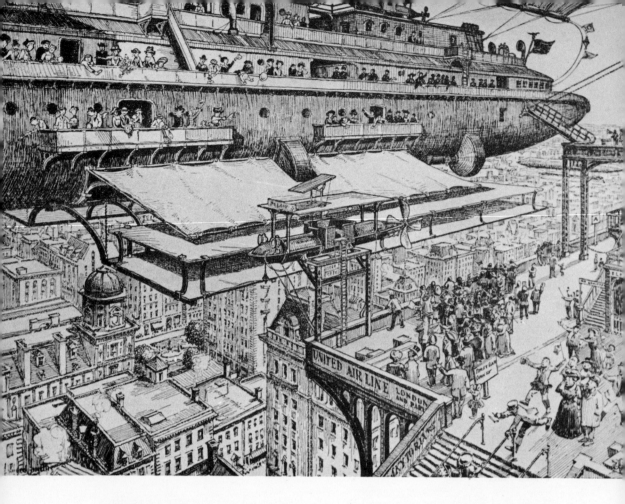

1910 LIFE

Above: A conception of today's United Air Line transatlantic airship. Here, passengers board the sky machine from the roof of a New York skyscraper.

1895 LIFE

Opposite page: A forecast of the status of the airplane in 1950. The illustration was captioned:

"Why, there goes a flying machine!"

"So it is. It's the first one I've seen in ten years. I can remember when the sky used to be covered with them. Curious how soon these fads die out."

1950.

1877 PUCK

Outdoor advertising will reach such a stage, that the Hudson River Palisades will soon look like this.

1883 JUDGE

"The School of the Future" was the title of this pro segregation cartoon.

1899 LIFE

Captioned "The Last American—1976," this picture shows the sole surviving Yankee attired in the apparel of his Colonial forefathers being ridiculed by the immigrants of many nations. Behind him stands the crumbling Federal Hall building, New York, where George Washington took the first oath of office.

1889 JUDGE

A club exclusively for ladies will soon become a reality . . . said *Judge* in 1889, and when it does this is what it will look like.

1856 HARPER'S NEW MONTHLY MAGAZINE

A hundred years ago *Harper's Magazine* peeked at the crystal ball to see what the well dressed man of the future would be wearing.

The businessman (*above, left*) will wear little clothing, said *Harper's*. Attached to the legs of his shorts will be "an interest table and a sailing schedule of the expresses for the various parts of the world." (Note the quill pen in his hat. The picture was drawn two years before the steel pen made its appearance.)

Next to him stands the more smartly attired "Man of Fashion" who, like the businessman, will be a citizen of the "Republic of United Interests."

1901 LIFE

Opposite page.

AMERICAN SUMMER FASHIONS FOR 1920.

1895 LIFE

This 1895 view of football of the future may be slightly exaggerated (no one has yet suffered decapitation on the field) but the conception of the giant stadium to come was not too far off. When the picture was drawn the giant concrete football stadium was unknown in America. The first one was built by Harvard University in 1904.

1904 LIFE

This is what the average college president will look like, when football
dominates our universities.

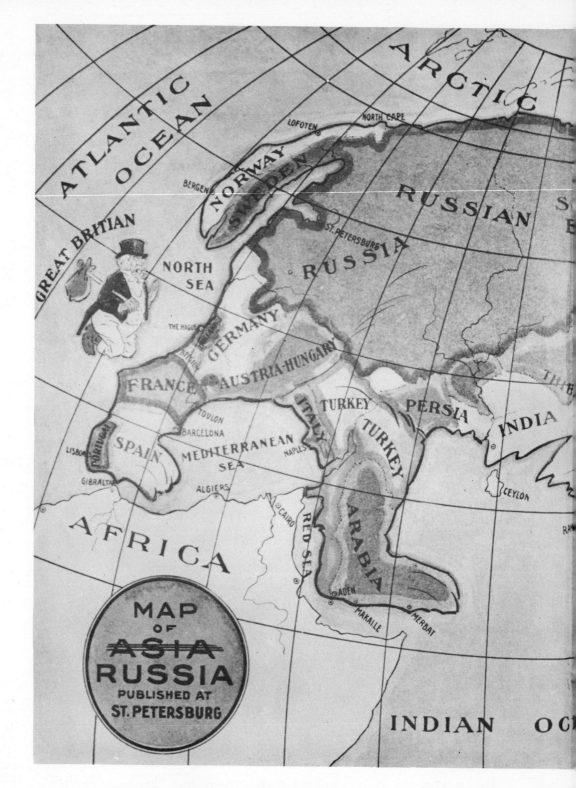

1904 JUDGE

A predatory, bear-shaped Russia absorbing the map of Asia and Europe

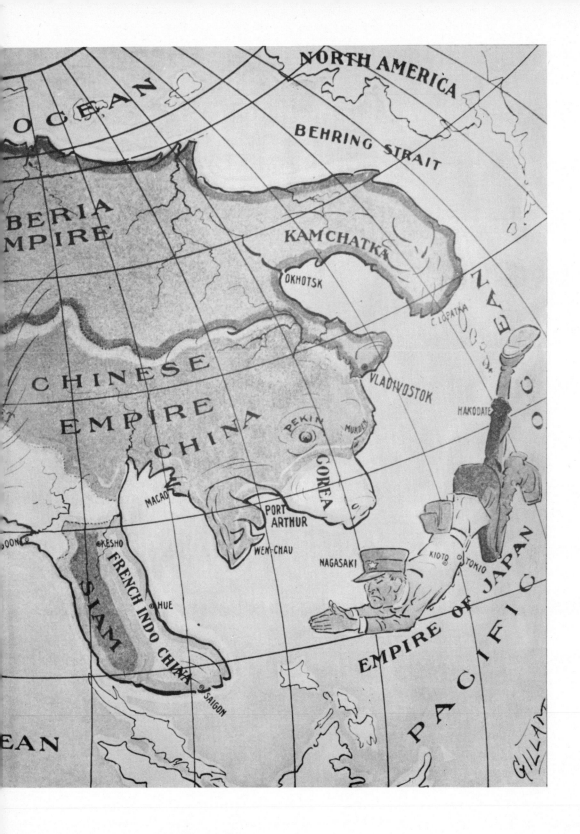

is this too-accurate-for-comfort prediction.

1913 LIFE

Tomorrow's luxury liner, as seen in 1913, will be a floating city, so huge that its decks will be thoroughfares crowded with shops, cafés, theaters and even trolley cars.

1913 JUDGE

Opposite page: "A diversion on the New York-Chicago air line—feeding the Allegheny eagles," was this crystal ball view of today's commercial air ship.

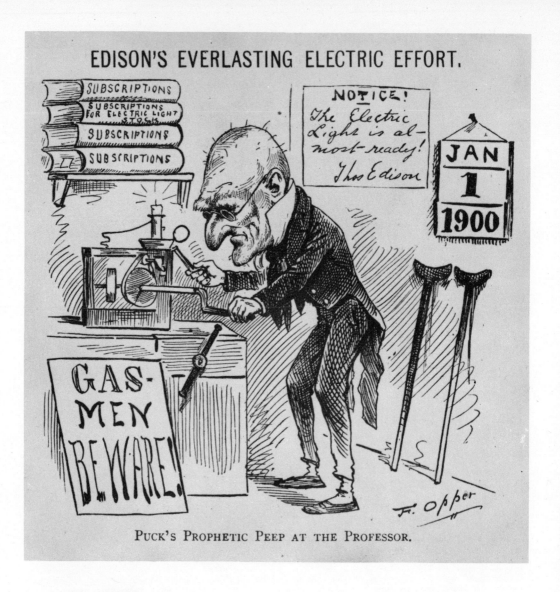

EDISON'S EVERLASTING ELECTRIC EFFORT.

SUBSCRIPTIONS
SUBSCRIPTIONS FOR ELECTRIC LIGHT STOCK
SUBSCRIPTIONS
SUBSCRIPTIONS

NOTICE! The Electric Light is almost ready! Thos Edison

JAN 1 1900

GAS-MEN BEWARE!

F. Opper

PUCK'S PROPHETIC PEEP AT THE PROFESSOR.

1882 PUCK

Cartoonist F. Opper saw Thomas A. Edison still working on his long promised electric light until 1900 with no results yet in sight. (Edison's first public demonstration of the light in 1879 caused gas stocks to tumble. He then turned his hand to producing dynamos to make his lighting system possible. Meanwhile impatient stockholders who had bought shares in Edison's company began to wonder if the electric light would ever become an actuality. Hence this satirical forecast.)

1882 PUCK

Opposite page: The sprinkler system as a means of putting out fires in theaters was foretold in this 1882 illustration.

1896 LIFE

Coins by the carriage load will be the result .

the Democrats' free coinage of silver program.

The Airship to Come

1878 CENTURY MAGAZINE

The "aeronon of the Twentieth Century" will be a fish-shaped machine of light metal, propelled by electric motors and will use a non-explosive gas for buoyancy, predicted *Century Magazine*. Capable of carrying numerous passengers and great cargoes, it will "travel 80 miles an hour in favorable winds, and reach Europe in a day and a half." (Dimensions: 300 feet long, 100 feet high amidships, 66 feet wide.) "The ends of the earth will be visited by all," the magazine stated. "An entirely new profession—that of airmanship—will be thoroughly organized, employing a countless army of airmen. . . . Boundaries will be obliterated. . . . The great peoples of Christendom will arrive at a common understanding; the Congress of Nations will no longer be an ideal scheme. . . . Troops, aerial squadrons, death-dealing armaments will be maintained only for police surveillance over barbarous races, and for instantly enforcing the judicial decrees of the world's international court of appeal." In closing the author darkly predicted that when the flying machine becomes a fact "the teeth of the railway managers will be drawn and the clippings of their claws will follow."

IN THE FUTURE.

STRANDED ON A DESERTED ASTEROID.

1906 LIFE

This picture does not seem so far fetched today in view of space-conquering rockets and the government's plan to launch an earth satellite within the next few years.

1856 HARPER'S NEW MONTHLY MAGAZINE

Above is an 1856 glimpse of the future airship. As the artist then saw it, the balloon-like craft would be kept on an even keel by wings and directed by a driver with reins. (Of interest is the artist's conception of the airship's fuselage, which is similar to the horse-drawn bus of the 1850's.)

1862 VANITY FAIR

The use of balloons in the Civil War (for observation purposes only)
undoubtedly inspired this cartoon, predicting that they would one day be
used as offensive weapons.

1878 NEW YORK DAILY GRAPHIC

A few men foresaw the controlled, elongated balloon before Count von Zeppelin began his experiments with the dirigible in 1895. An early believer in the future of that type of flying machine was Professor C. F. Ritchell, who came up with the above conception in 1878.

1896 NEW YORK HERALD

This is the future battleship of the clouds, said the *New York Herald* sixty years ago. The giant boat-shaped car (100 feet long, 50 feet wide and 25 feet deep) will be supported by five huge balloons, propelled by sails and will carry 125 men. A crew of only five men will be needed to operate this "greyhound of the air," enthused the *Herald*. There will be no danger of fire aboard for the great craft will be "electrically operated." Water will be taken on from the clouds. The airship will hover over the enemy above the reach of the most powerful ground artillery and dynamite bombs will then be released.

(The airship was designed by a Dr. Wells of St. Louis for the supposed purpose of aiding the Cuban insurrectionists. Needless to say, it never got off the ground.)

1898 LIFE

This illustration, captioned "Glimpses of the Future—Snapshot of Upper Fifth Avenue in 1930," is one of the earliest conceptions of the heavier-than-air flying machine.

1909 LIFE

Long before the municipal airport was known, artist W. Terry drew this picture which was captioned: "A Bird's-Eye View—The Near Future."

1907 LIFE

"The Regatta of the Future" actually came to pass in 1920 when the first intercollegiate air meet was staged on Long Island. Among the college entries were Yale and Harvard, first honors going to Yale.

1903 JUDGE

Above is a 1903 New York Central Railroad advertisement which suggested that the airship (a dirigible) might some day prove a faster means of travel than the line's crack train on the New York-Chicago run.

A SHIPWRECK OF THE FUTURE.
"TO THE PARACHUTES!"

1911 JUDGE

"A Precaution Which Will Soon Be Necessary," was the caption of this illustration.

1902 LIFE

Over fifty years ago cartoonist Rudolph Dirks offered this version of a future aerial disaster.

1909 LIFE

Cartoonist Carey came close to hitting the bull's-eye with this sketch of the rain makers to come. The caption: "Hey, Boys, round up this flock of clouds and drive 'em over to Haskill's ranch. He's ordered rain for 5 o'clock this afternoon."

1909 JUDGE

Farming by plane is now commonplace but it was unknown in 1909 when this cartoon was published. *"How It Will Be Done,"* ran the caption. "Now steer over the 40-acre corn patch and we'll get it planted after breakfast."

LOST IN THE YEAR 1925 A. D.

ADRIFT IN THE GREAT CANYONS OF NEW YORK CITY

1909 LIFE

These two tongue-in-cheek forecasts were not too far off the beam at that.

Above, left: A dirigible delivers air mail while in flight over Omaha. (A similar event took place on July 15, 1928, when an Air Corps dirigible transferred a sack of mail to a moving train at Belleville, Illinois.)

The other picture brings to mind the disaster of July 28, 1945, when a B-25 bomber crashed into New York's Empire State Building, killing thirteen people.

"TAXI!"

1915 LIFE

A double header is this cartoon, predicting for 1950 (a) the air taxi and (b) the subordination of the American husband.

1906 LIFE

This view of the air taxi to come shows the streets of New York devoid of traffic.

1913 PUCK

"For the Sunny South—An Airship With a Jim Crow Trailer," was the caption of this cartoon.

1911 LIFE

Astonishing is the above preview of an air attack at sea and the use of the naval anti-aircraft gun—a generation before such an event took place.

1912 LIFE

Below: This forecast brings to mind the series of man-made islands which are now being constructed off the Atlantic coastline.

1915

A MID-ATLANTIC FUEL DEPOT

1912 LIFE

Round-the-world airplane flights will take place in 1920, stated the caption of this 1912 illustration. (The prognosticator was only four years off. The first world flight was achieved in 1924 when two U. S. Army planes circled the globe on an eastward course which began and ended at Seattle, Washington.)

1912 LIFE

Harry Grant Dart, whose elaborate portrayals of future scenes and events frequently enlivened the pages of *Life* and *Judge* from about 1910 to 1930, drew this conception of a World Series, as of today.

THE HORSESHOE IN 2000 A.D.

AËROPLANIST. — What is it? Can you make out?

HIS MECHANICIAN. — Give it up. Must be a part of some early type of motor.

1913 PUCK

This scene may come to pass but it is doubtful if the flying machine in 2000 A.D. will look like the pre-World War I model shown here.

Tomorrow's Auto

1896 JUDGE

This fanciful conception of the horseless age to come may be the first cartoon of an automobile to appear in an American periodical. (In 1896 the foremost automobile manufacturers in this country were the Duryea brothers of Springfield, Massachusetts, who produced a total of ten cars that year.)

1901 LIFE

Opposite page: This cartoon was titled "A Prediction For 1905. Of course there will always be some use for the automobile." Cartoonist Kemble, who thought that the auto would pass out of existence by 1905 and be replaced by the airship (note the model) was gazing into a cloudy crystal ball. (By 1905 the number of registered cars in the United States had grown to a total of 77,988.)

Kemble.

1902 LIFE

"This will be the next step if the American family means to protect itself," was the caption of this 1902 anti-auto cartoon.

1904 LIFE

Opposite page: The devastation to come with the automobile at large is shown in this picture. (In 1904 accidents were occurring with such frequency that New York State passed a law limiting the speed of autos to ten miles an hour in congested areas, fifteen miles an hour in villages and twenty miles an hour on country roads.)

THE AUTOMOBILE OF THE FUTURE.

1904 LIFE

This multiple-decked monster of the future recalls the top heavy Fifth Avenue buses of the Twenties and Thirties.

1906 LIFE

Not too far off was this prediction of the house trailer to come.

1901 JUDGE

These costumes, hermetically sealed and warranted dust proof, will be *de rigeur* for motorists in the future, said *Judge* in 1901. At that time there were but a few miles of paved roads in the United States and many considered the automobile a dust-making nuisance.

1905 LIFE

Opposite page: According to this glimpse of life in 2005, the automobile will be king and the horse will have degenerated to the size of a lap dog.

IN A THOUSAND YEARS

Above: **1905 JUDGE**

Below: **1913 JUDGE**

Safety devices for tomorrow's pedestrian, as *Judge* saw it.

YOUNG AMERICA IN THE NEAR FUTURE.

1908 LIFE

The hot rod vogue among today's teen-agers was foreseen with considerable clarity in this 1908 cartoon.

1911 LIFE

The drive-in church service, now commonplace throughout the United States, was foreseen by cartoonist George Carlson in 1911—some thirty years before the first one took place.

1901 JUDGE

Above: The motorized farm combine of the future.

1911 LIFE

Below: Tomorrow's limousine with separate compartments for servants, nursery, secretary, office, den, library and kitchenette.

1913 LIFE

The modern superhighway with its elaborate interchange system was foreseen to a measurable degree by illustrator Arthur Lewis in 1913.

Glimpses of the City of the Future

1881 HARPER'S WEEKLY

In the 1880's before electricity went underground, life in the city was perilous because of the maze of wires strung on telegraph poles which stood as thick as trees in a forest. If this state of affairs continues, commented *Harper's Weekly*, this is what we may expect.

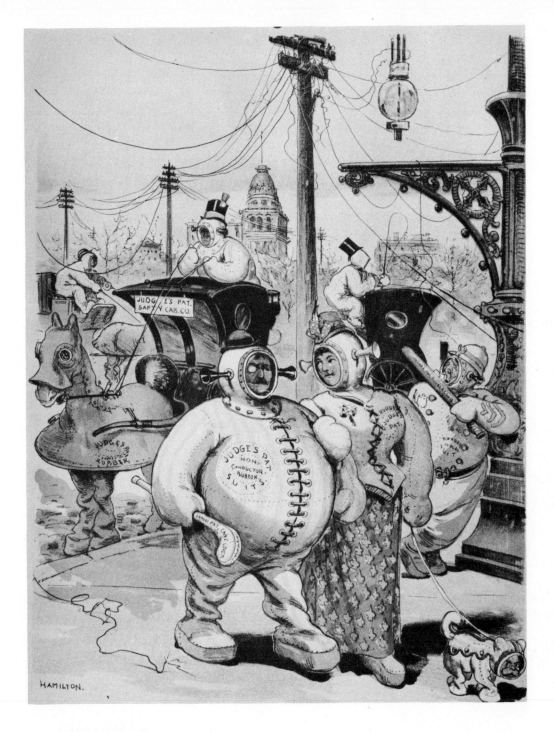

1889 JUDGE

The live wire menace inspired this 1889 cartoon which shows citizens of the future attired in rubber clothing for protection.

1875 HARPER'S WEEKLY

A photograph taken today of Trinity Church, New York, would be strikingly similar to this sketch drawn in 1875, when the church towered above all other buildings in the city.

1898 LIFE

This picture captioned "A Sunny Day in 1910," was drawn in 1898, before the age of the skyscraper.

1901 JUDGE

This pair of cartoons shows (*left*) a recently erected statue of a great American, and (*right*) how the statue will look in the future when the growing city engulfs it.

1883 FRANK LESLIE'S ILLUSTRATED NEWSPAPER

The picture below was inspired by the great floods of 1883 which inundated the cities of Toledo, Louisville and Cincinnati.

SAFETY AGAINST FLOODS—THE WESTERN CITY OF THE FUTURE.

1884 JUDGE

The vertical growth of New York with an increasing number of "L" lines extending above the highest buildings was foreseen in this illustration.

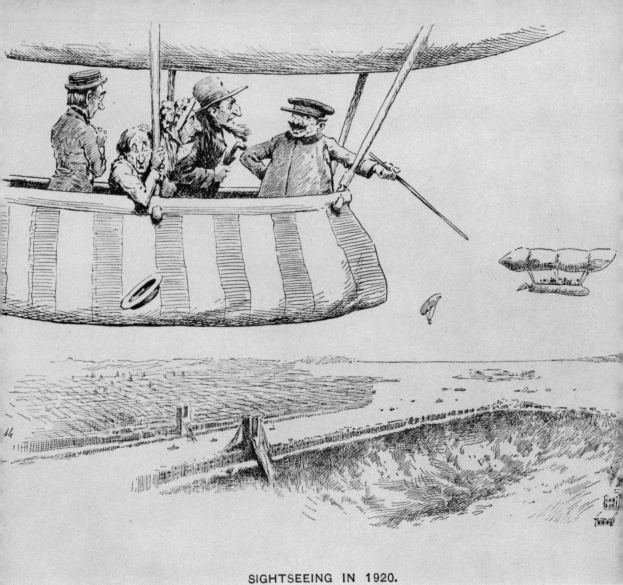

SIGHTSEEING IN 1920.

1902 LIFE

"That depression down there is where New York City stood. But with all its skyscrapers and underground tunnels it suddenly sunk one day and they haven't been able to find it since."

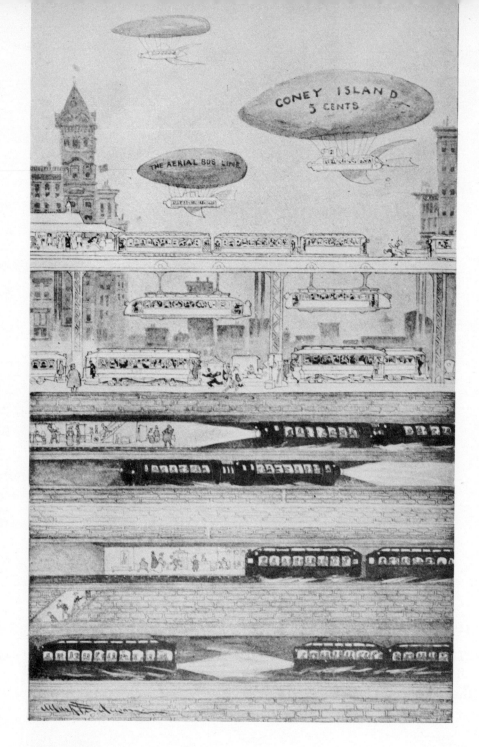

1908 LIFE

A sectional view of the city of the future.

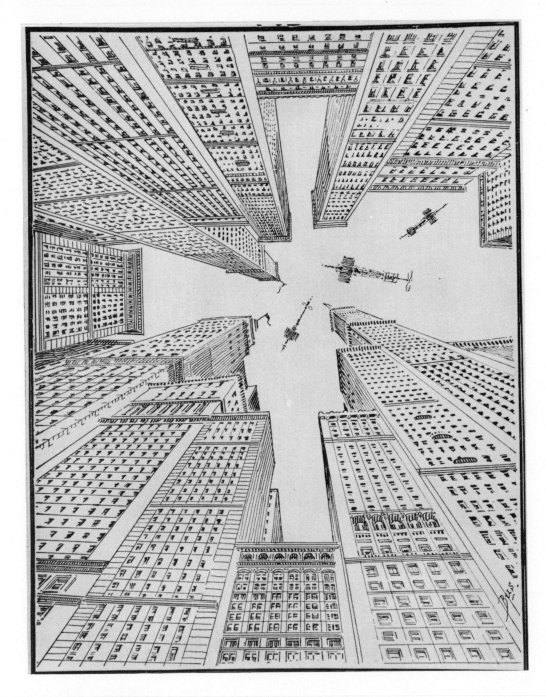

1911 JUDGE

This picture was captioned "Aviation of the 21st Century."

1903 LIFE

The erection of the Flatiron Building in 1902, New York's first skyscraper, gave rise to many cartoons of the future city. An example is the above conception titled, "Now John, don't lose that parachute. It's the only decent one I have."

1909 LIFE

Opposite page: Long before the penthouse became a part of city life, cartoonist A. B. Walker looked ahead and saw country homes in the sky.

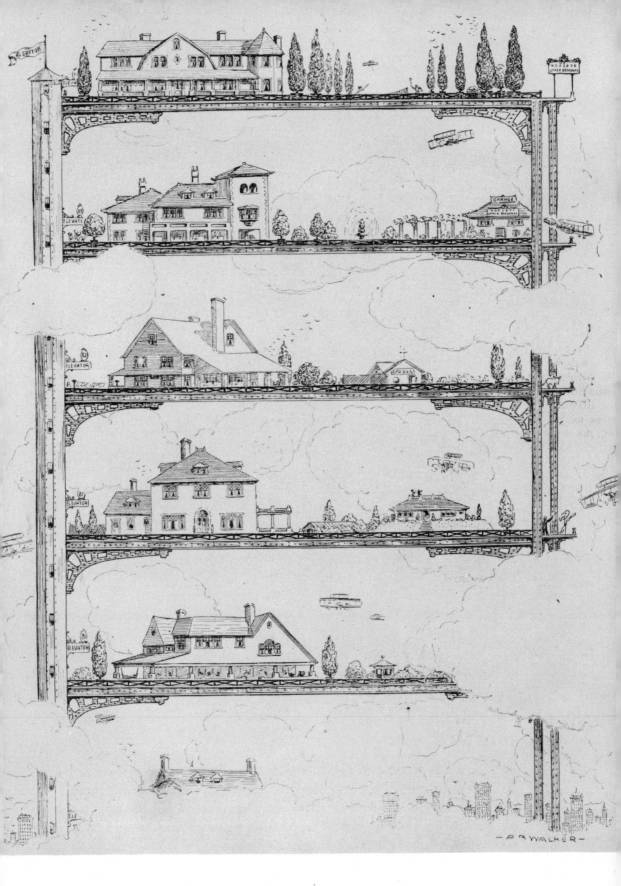

1910 LIFE

New York City in the late Twentieth Century, according to this view, will be crowned with elevated boulevards, cable-suspended express trains, places of amusement like ball parks, swimming pools and theaters, and air stations from which it will be possible to board airships and fly to Chicago in six hours, to California in twenty hours.

THE 20 HOUR
FLIER
TO CALIFORNIA

6 HOURS
TO CHICAGO
BY THE RED FLIERS

ELEVATORS TO
BOULEVARD

R. G.
RUSSOM.

THE NEXT STEP.

If the Bike Craze Continues

1896 LIFE

The Gay Nineties was the day of the bicycle. At first a mild fad, bicycling became almost a national craze. Manufacturers sold over 1,000,000 bikes a year and still there were not enough to meet the demand. More complicated machines appeared: the tandem for two, the triplet, the quadruplet and finally one to end all—a 13-seater.

A multi-cycle that was never manufactured is the two-decker shown above but, as the caption indicates, it might come to pass anytime in the near future.

1899 LIFE

What will surely happen if the bike craze is not brought under control,
was the theme of this illustration.

1896 LIFE

"For the souls of the wheelers—to those countless bicyclists who insist upon their Sunday a.m. outing," a church service on wheels will be the solution, stated the caption of this cartoon.

1897 LIFE

"In the Future—no more equestrian statues for our distinguished men," was the title of this cartoon.

1896 NEW YORK HERALD

Opposite page: This peep into the future shows the effeminacy of the American male, made so by the bloomer-wearing women wheelers.

A PEEP INTO THE FUTURE.

Sports and Higher Learning

1911 LIFE

From the 1880's, when football first became popular, until just before World War I, a favorite theme of the cartoonists of the era was the overemphasis of sports in our colleges and the consequent decline of learning.

An example is the above conception of a college seal of the future bearing an emblem which translated, means: To Hell With Wisdom.

1886 PUCK

Above: "Sketch of a college commencement as it will be when the great athletic idea in education has done its work."

1887 LIFE

Below: A headline that one may expect to see in the near future.

EXTRA!

YALE vs. PRINCETON

AT FOOTBALL.

ONLY THIRTY LIVES LOST!

SIXTEEN WOUNDED!

1888 LIFE

"The Art Museum of the Future," will be devoted entirely to exhibits of sports and athletics, predicted Charles Dana Gibson in 1888.

THE
S'LUGGER

1903 LIFE

Above: "What the Game Will Come To."

1896 LIFE

Below: Football styles of the future.

1906 JUDGE

So numerous were football casualties in 1905 (18 deaths and 149 serious injuries) that new rules to de-brutalize the game and make it more open were put into effect the following season. The changes were generally approved, but not by *Judge* which ridiculed the idea and saw the future game degenerating into something like a tea party between two effeminate dudes.

1884 JUDGE

The new protective equipment for the baseball catcher will eventually result in this, according to *Judge*.

OUR NATIONAL GAME IN 2005 A. D.

1905 LIFE

A thousand years hence (said *Life* in 1905) America's national game will be played the world over and teams will consist of players representing every nationality.

When Women Get Their Rights

1905 LIFE

The rise of feminism was a popular theme among cartoonists from the time Amelia Bloomer launched her campaign for women's dress reform in 1851 until about 1920 when women at last got the vote.

The above sketch of tomorrow's woman was drawn in 1905, when ladies did not smoke or wear slacks.

1897 LIFE

Opposite page: "An Inauguration of the Future."

1896 LIFE

"The New Navy—about 1900 A.D." was the title of this cartoon.

1897 LIFE

Above: "Is this to be the bald-headed row of the future?"

1910 LIFE

Below: "When our railroads are run by the fair sex."

IN 1920

GOVERNESS O'TOOLE OF NEW YORK ATTENDS DRILL AT THE MILITARY ACADEMY, WEST POINT

1912 LIFE

New York has yet to have a woman governor, as cartoonist Otho Cushing predicted (*above*), but the same cannot be said of Wyoming and Texas, which states elected Mrs. Nellie G. Ross and Mrs. Miriam "Ma" Ferguson respectively to gubernatorial honors in 1925.

1912

INTERIOR OF THE OFFICE OF PERKINS, SISTER & CO.

1908 LIFE

In 1908 illustrator James Montgomery Flagg saw women taking over the business world by 1912 with these results.

1916 LIFE

As the woman suffrage movement gained full momentum during Wilson's administration the cartoonists of the day tended to make the male more effeminate than ever, the female more masculine. An example is the above cartoon, titled "When Women Do the Fighting."

Forecasts from
the Grab Bag

1878 PUCK

The new fangled telephone of the 1870's
inspired this cartoon in which a colonel
of the future is seen directing from afar
an attack upon the enemy.

1885 LIFE

The Sunday morning service in times to come will be broadcast by a preacher sitting in his chair at home, said *Life* in 1885.

1887 NEW YORK DAILY GRAPHIC

Opposite page: Events that will come to pass when the telephone is established. From *top to bottom:* a musical broadcast; an organ recital to an unseen audience; an interview by telephone.

A MUSIC MILL FOR ALL THE THEATRES.

INTERVIEWING PER TELEPHONE

103

1891 LIFE
Above: An American landscape of the future.

1893 LIFE
Below: A glimpse of sky-writing to come.

1885 PUCK

Advertising in the near future.

1904 LIFE

A view of sky advertising as it will be.

1917 LIFE

American scenery as future motorists will see it.

THE "BRITISH TAR" OF THE FUTURE.

1862 PUNCH

In April, 1862, a month after the first battle of ironclads (the *Monitor* and the *Merrimac*), *Punch* published this cartoon, predicting that armor would be worn by the British tar of the future.

WAR DEP'T
BULLETIN

PHILIPPINE REBELS
ROUTED !!!

AGUINALDO IV
TRAPPED !!!

HIS CAPTURE AND THE
COMPLETE PACIFICATION
OF THE ISLANDS NOW A
QUESTION OF BUT A
FEW DAYS

IN 1950.

1900 LIFE

In the above satirical cartoon, *Life* looked ahead fifty years and saw American forces still pursuing the Filipino rebel, Emilio Aguinaldo.

(Aguinaldo, who had led an insurrection against the Spaniards, turned against America following our conquest of the Philippines. For more than two years his guerilla bands eluded pursuing U. S. forces. As the chase dragged on Americans at home began to wonder if Aguinaldo wouldn't remain at large indefinitely, despite optimistic bulletins issued by the War Department. He was finally captured, however, in March, 1901.)

Of interest is the artist's conception of 1950 styles, the automobile and the airship.

1915 LIFE

This picture was published during the second year of World War I.
The caption: "TOURISTS OF 1920. The guide: 'This was Europe.'"

1916 LIFE

If America does not go to war against Germany, warned *Life*, this is what the map of North America will look like.

1917 LIFE

A more dramatic view of what will happen if America continues to remain neutral is shown in the above picture.

1918 LIFE

A new Germany more powerful and more warlike than ever will rise again to oppose the Allies in "1935 or thereabouts unless the job is finished now," warned cartoonist Walker with remarkable foresight.

Held in New York Times

A bartender of the future

1919 LIFE

Cartoonists had a field day on the eve of National Prohibition. Among them was John Held, Jr. (*above*), who wrongly predicted that the future bartender would be limited to serving non-alcoholic drinks.

(Wrong also was Daniel C. Roper, Commissioner of Internal Revenue, who predicted that the Prohibition Law "will be enforced and will result in a nation that knows no alcohol.")

1919 LIFE

More accurate was this glimpse of what prohibition would lead to.

("Rum Row," a strip some twenty miles off the Atlantic seaboard frequented by liquor-smuggling vessels, was not established until the mid-Twenties.)

1919 LIFE

Although the dirigible was never used to smuggle liquor during prohibition the airplane was frequently employed to fly booze into the United States from Canada, Mexico and Cuba.

THE GREAT EXODUS OF 1925

1919 LIFE

Cartoonist R. B. Fuller's prediction that the increasing number of blue laws would cause a great exodus from the United States is not too absurd when it is recalled that hordes of thirsty citizens fled the country during the Twenties.

1900 SCIENTIFIC AMERICAN

The four-day transatlantic liner will some day be built, predicted the *Scientific American* in 1900. The dimensions and speed of the magazine's ship of the future are not too far from those of the S.S. *United States*, today's superliner.

The liner to be: length, 930 feet; beam, 87 feet; displacement, 40,000 tons; speed, 30 knots; horse power, 110,000.

The *United States:* length, 990 feet; beam, 101½ feet; speed, 35 knots plus. (Displacement and horsepower are listed as classified information.)

Way off was the *Scientific American* on the probable cost of such a liner: $6,000,000. The *United States* cost more than $70,000,000.

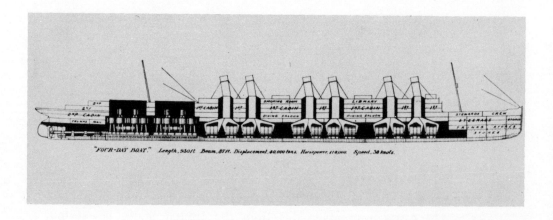

"FOUR-DAY BOAT." Length, 930 ft. Beam, 87 ft. Displacement, 40,000 tons. Horsepower, 110,000. Speed, 30 knots.

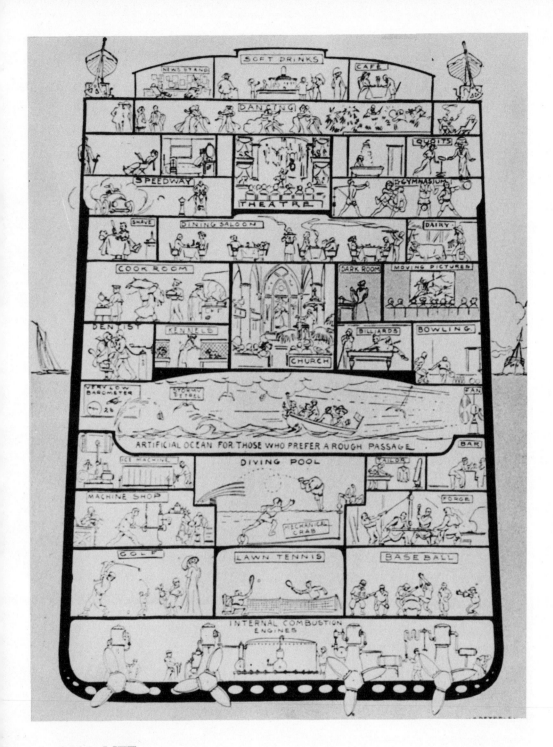

1911 LIFE

Less scientific was this conception of the liner of tomorrow.

1907 JUDGE

"If they keep on building steamships larger."

1902 LIFE

In 1902, the year before the Wright brothers made the first airplane flight and eight years before the first wireless message was sent from a plane, the above cartoon appeared in *Life*. The caption: "Confound this wireless telegraphy. My wife has been calling me ever since I left home."

1911 LIFE

Wireless, according to this fanciful view, will be more than a means of communication in the future. It will enable aircraft to course the skys on a network of invisible tracks—a conception somewhat akin to ground-guided aircraft of today.

1893 LIFE

Above: The postage stamp of the future—an anti-immigration cartoon.

1892 JUDGE

Below: "In the Near Future—Fifth Avenue on St. Pat's Day."

1902 LIFE

"Washington's Birthday in New York," was the caption of this cartoon predicting that the Germans would soon take over the city. (In 1902 some three million people of German birth were residing in this country.)

THE AMERICAN FOURTH OF THE FUTURE.

1890 LIFE

Among the fashionable set in the latter part of the Nineteenth Century it was considered ultra smart to admire and imitate all things British, much to the disgust of the average American. Hence, the above satirical cartoon.

1915 LIFE

"The Theatrical Season of 2001," was the title of this cartoon.

1897 LIFE

"The lynching game of the future. During recess the southern schoolboys of the next generation may indulge in this sort of fun."

HARVARD'S FOOTBALL ELEVEN OF 1909, UNDER PRESIDENT ROOSEVELT, OF HARVARD.

1904 LIFE

This cartoon, drawn by James Montgomery Flagg, was inspired by the appearance of a Negro on the 1904 Harvard football team. (He was William Matthews, a left end.)

The allusion to Roosevelt in the caption undoubtedly stems from the fact that the President in 1901 invited Negro educator Booker T. Washington to lunch at the White House, an act that scandalized the South.

131

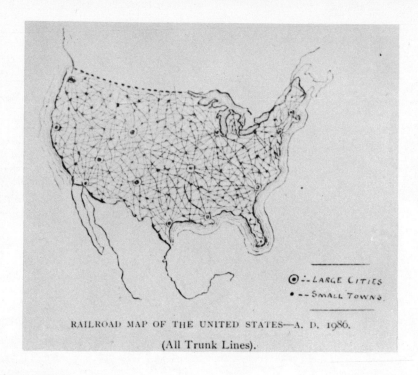

RAILROAD MAP OF THE UNITED STATES—A. D. 1986.

(All Trunk Lines).

1890 LIFE

The railroads will so overrun the country by 1986, said *Life* in 1890, that the United States will be a network of tracks (*above*) and the countryside will be despoiled, as seen below.

And, of course, by that time, everything will be in such a condition that Fashionable Society will welcome him with open arms.

F. Opper

1886 PUCK

"THE AMERICAN WORKINGMAN OF THE FUTURE—when the labor agitators have 'improved his condition' until he is perfectly satisfied with it. And, of course, by that time, everything will be in such condition that Fashionable Society will welcome him with open arms."

1856 HARPER'S NEW MONTHLY MAGAZINE

These sketches of a hundred years ago predicted (*above*) "The Infantine Ward," in which tube-fed babies "will be reared from their birth" and (*below*) the remodeling of the human face. Thus did *Harper's* foresee by many years the incubator for infants and plastic surgery.

1883 FRANK LESLIE'S ILLUSTRATED NEWSPAPER

Back in the 1880's Chicago had already established itself as a leading crime center, if this cartoon is to be believed. Entitled "What it is coming to in Chicago," the sketch suggested a protective costume for evening wear in the Windy City.

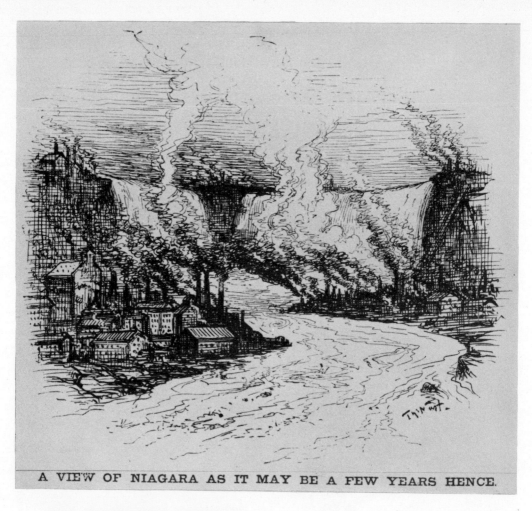

A VIEW OF NIAGARA AS IT MAY BE A FEW YEARS HENCE.

1883 HARPER'S WEEKLY

So far Niagara Falls has not yet come to this but there are many who fear that it is still a possibility.

1897 LIFE

"Probabilities for 1947. Queen Victoria and the Prince of Wales."

When Hy Mayer drew this cartoon in 1897 the Queen had been on the throne for 60 years, the Prince (later Edward VII) was a chubby, middle aged man of 56, and it seemed then that she might reign forever.

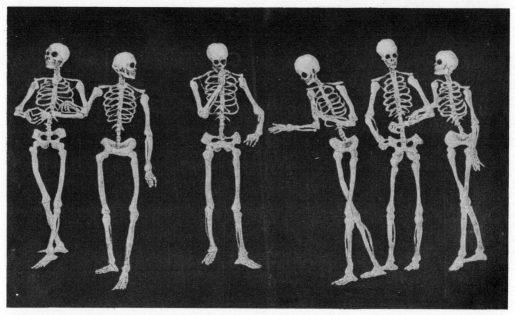

1896 LIFE

Roentgen's announced discovery of X-rays in 1895 led to all sorts of speculations, among them this prediction by illustrator Charles Dana Gibson who wondered if a new kind of photography might not be the result.

1897 LIFE

"Glimpses of the Future. The Stage in the Twentieth Century, as Promised by Present Indications."

1902 JUDGE

Demanding servants will soon result in the mass migration of harassed householders to the ease and comfort of the hotel and apartment, said *Judge* in 1902.

1907 LIFE

Above: A view of the suburbs of the future, when pedestrians will be forced off the highways by the increasing number of vehicles.

1913 PUCK

Opposite page: "Museum Attendant (in 1925): 'These instruments, known as stock tickers, were in use in Wall Street up to the year 1914. They were abandoned when the public got out of the market, and they are now very rare.'"

THE FUTURE OF THE TICKER.

143

1903 LIFE

The munificence of Andrew Carnegie who gave millions to libraries and other institutions, many of which bore his name, inspired these critical sketches.

1911 LIFE

Above is cartoonist Walker's conception of the stained glass enshrinement of John D. Rockefeller in the church of the future.

The World To-morrow

The Taj Mahal Motion Picture Palace—Main Street—Agra, India

1920 LIFE

A look-ahead at the Hollywood influence, as seen by cartoonist Rea Irvin.

1922 LIFE

"THE LAST HORSE," an event that will soon come to pass.

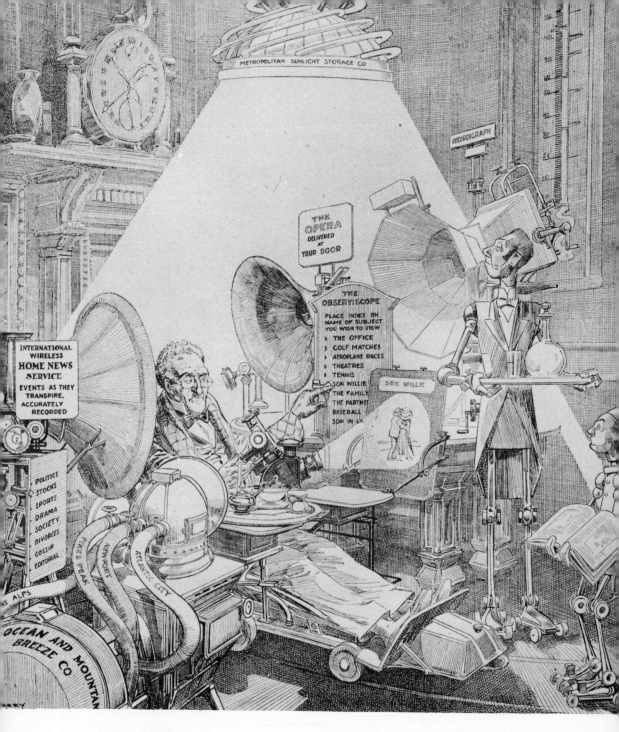

1911 LIFE

By stretching the imagination a little it can be said that Harry Grant
Dart, who drew this cartoon in 1911, predicted the radio, television, the
sun lamp and air conditioning. His robot servant, however, has not yet
been perfected.

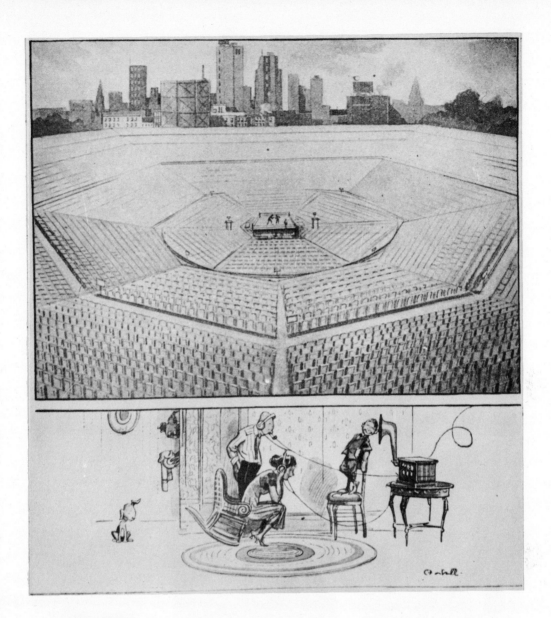

1923 LIFE

The radio, said *Life* in the days of the crystal set, will have this result on the boxing game.

DR. HENRY M. LEETZ, OF THE STATE BUREAU OF TEETH PREVENTION, SHOWING HOW TO BRUSH TEETH THE WRONG WAY.

HON. GEORGE NOTWILER TALKING.

HON. HERMAN KALUF TALKING.

MISS MATTIE EARL, OF THE NEEDLE-WORK GUILD, DOING FILET WORK.

EARL CHAMLE, OF THE GOVERNMENT LOCUST SERVICE, TEACHING A LOCUST HOW TO WALK.

SECRETARY NAMAMY TALKING.

1924 LIFE

The above preview of the horrors of television to come was conceived fifteen years before the first public TV demonstration.

1929 JUDGE

Looking ahead several years, *Judge* in 1929 saw television and the telephone combined (*as above*) with unfortunate results. The caption:

A POSSIBLE DRAWBACK OF TELEVISION

"Central, you've given me the wrong number!"

"Excuse it, please."